Music Through the Ages

OrangeBooks Publication

1st Floor, Rajhans Arcade, Mall Road, Kohka, Bhilai, Chhattisgarh 490020

Website: **www.orangebooks.in**

© Copyright, 2024, Author

All rights reserved. No part of this book may be reproduced, stored in a retrieval system, or transmitted, in any form by any means, electronic, mechanical, magnetic, optical, chemical, manual, photocopying, recording or otherwise, without the prior written consent of its writer.

First Edition, 2024

ISBN: 978-93-5621-423-1

Music Through The Ages

A Concise View to Music History

ASHOK G P

Orange Books Publication
www.orangebooks.in

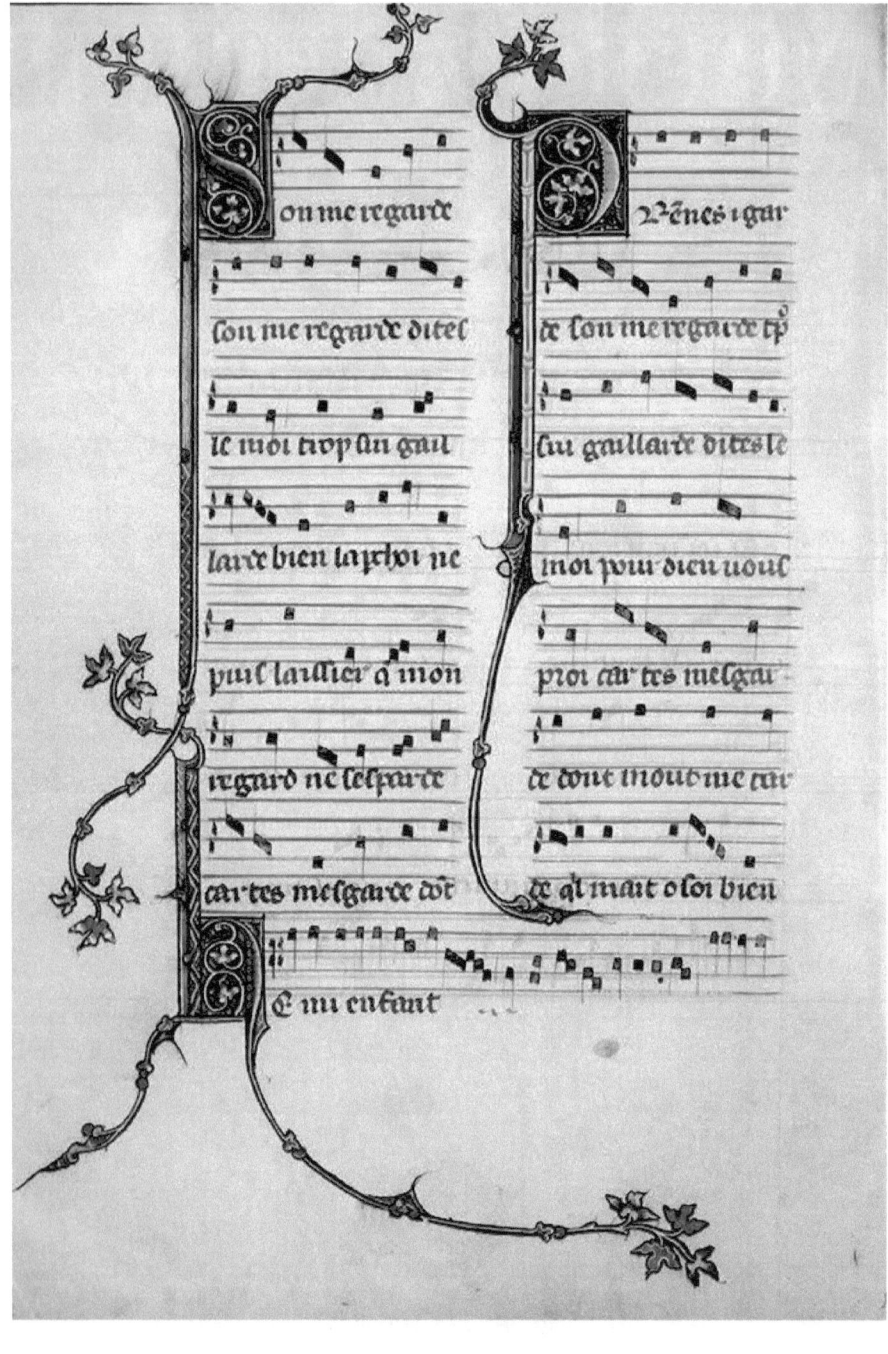

Table of Contents

An Introduction to Music 1

Ancient Music 3500 B.C – 300 A.D (Outline) 2

Middle Ages 400 A.D – 1400 A.D 4

Renaissance 1400 A.D – 1600 A.D 8

Baroque Era 1600 A.D - 1750 A.D 15

The Classical Era 1750 A.D - 1827 A.D 25

Romantic Era 1827 A.D - 1900 A.D 32

The Twentieth Century Modern Era 1900 A.D - 1990 A.D 37

Glossary of Musical Terms 45

About the Author 67

♫

An Introduction to Music

We have heard it, felt it, and enjoyed it, but when it comes to coherently stating it, we stutter.

Some say it is a feeling, while others say it is a language however:

Music – is organized sound that fills up time, and eventually the space in terms of the ambiance in its surroundings.

Music, unlike any other art form, encapsulates the ear and pierces right into the soul. It is an art form that truly embodies the celestial, wraps in the earthly essence and transcends into the human psyche.

Regardless of how one relates to music, it has always been an enchanting endeavor for human society, shaping its course over millennia.

Some of the areas it has helped infiltrate are the philosophy of ancient civilizations, the chants of the temples across various faiths, and societies under dictatorial oppression.

Therefore, it has helped build and break down the seen & the unseen and the heard & the unheard.

Music has existed before the advent of humanity and will remain after the extinction of humanity.

Music was, is and will be

-Ashok G P

Western Music History
Ancient Music 3500 B.C – 300 A.D (Outline)

Sources

Our search for the earliest sources of Western music will take us back to ancient Greece, Rome and Egypt. Prehistoric societies developed instruments, pitches, melodies and rhythms. Early civilizations used music in religious ceremonies, to accompany dancing, for recreation, and in education, much as we do today.

Ancient writers directly influenced our way of thinking about music, from concepts such as notes, intervals, and scales, to notions of how music affects our feeling and character.

Music in the ancient world was essentially an oral tradition. Though the tradition is long and rich, only about 40 fragments of music have survived. Some sources of Ancient Music include pictures, paintings, and artifacts that depict musicians and their instruments, as well as fragments of instruments, anecdotal references in literature and a few theoretical treatises concerning music.

In the Bible, David, Asaph, Jeduthun, Heman, Solomon, and many others played instruments and sang. Full-time musician priests led worship through music in the temple. The psalms are the top 150 songs practiced and played by the people of Israel from about 1500 BC to about 600 BC.

Study of tribes less touched by the development of modern culture – such as those in Africa, Polynesia and extant practices of Native American Indian tribes reveals important insights.

References

Some Theoretical treatises concerning music would include:

Pythagoras 582 BC - 500 BC

Plato 427 BC - 347 BC - Timaeus, Republic.

Aristotle 384 BC - 322 BC - Politics.

Aristoxenus 354 BC - Harmonic Elements and Elements of Rhythmics.

Ceonides 1st century AD - Harmonic Introduction.

Aristeded Qintillianus c.200 AD - De Musica Libri VII

Athenaeus c.200 AD - Mentions musical performances in his books.

Music in the Ancient Era

All of the treatises describe music as a part of other art forms, whether religious, political, or dramatic. Music was not thought of as a separate entity from these other social structures.

All of the early forms appear to be improvisational, without set forms.

Music notation did not exist. Musical forms and practices were passed from one generation to the next through oral tradition.

There has been no written notation for Chinese music until recent centuries and some African tribal musical traditions, do not have a written form to this day.

Study: - *Petros Tabouris – Stasimon / Hurrian Hymn no 6 / Sarcophagus Lament / Epitaph dei Seikilos / Enki's Hailstorm*

Instruments of the Ancient Era

Harp

Lyre

Citole

Aulos

Phorminx

Middle Ages 400 A.D – 1400 A.D

Introduction

The Middle Ages in Western Music is approximately dated between the 4th Century A.D – 1400 A.D. During this period, a notational system was developed making it possibly the biggest step towards a standardized musical system. Music could now be taught, practiced and performed exactly as intended, in contrast to ancient music which differed between people and regions due to the oral system of music education.

600 – 1000 A.D.

Study: *- Ambrosian Chant – Ecce Apertum est Templum / Letentur Celi et Exultet Terra / Puer Natus est Nobis /*

The Medieval era saw the development of **Plainsong**, also referred to as the Plainchant, or Gregorian chant. Some characteristics of the Plainsong:

The Plainsong was monophonic (single texture), modal s (written in modes), sung acapella, non-metric, conjunct and finally sung in Latin.

Chants were basically of three types: Antiphonal (alternating choirs), Responsorial (alternating soloist and choir), or Direct (without alteration).

At least by the 9th Century (the 800's) **Organum** (plainsong with harmony) was developed. The first type of organum was called parallel or strict organum. The melody was the **Tenor** or **Vox Principalis** and the harmony was the **Duplum** or **Vox organalis.**

Study: *- Pascha Nostrum Organum Duplum – Leonin*

Free Organum developed as a more polyphonic technique starting with **Oblique motion** (one voice stayed on the same pitch while the other moved) and settling in with **Contrary Motion.**

Study*: - Leonin Perotin – Viderunt Omnes*

735 A.D

The **Monochord** was developed—an instrument similar to the Guitar, but with only one note being played at a time. Tuning was precise, and the instrument helped train singers and tune other instruments (this was a re-creation of what medieval intellectuals thought may have been the design of Pythagoras' original monochord).

800 A.D

Polyphony began when more notes were being sounded simultaneously and each note having its own melodic identity... An Irish Scholar, Guido, developed the Musica Enchiriadis. The musical instruction manual discusses a system based on the tetrachord of the finals, plainchant, and parallel organum.

Study: - *Ave Maris Stella – Himno En Honor*

700 – 1100 A.D

Monasteries were the central loci of musical instruction. **Tropes** (new music and words were added to the liturgy of the church).

Sequences (another portion added to the official liturgical chant, usually after the alleluia with text) and **Liturgical Dramas** (special music to liturgical texts usually for Easter or Christmas).

Conductus (a song for one or more voices with a serious sacred text in rhythmical Latin verse), and **Clausulae** (a cadence-an ending formula) were developed.

1000 A.D

A four-line **staff** was developed to help represent the movement of pitches; this was the beginning of a standard music notation system.

Study: - *Hildegard of Bingen – In Principio Omnes*

1100 – 1200 A.D

During this time **Cathedral Schools** replaced Monasteries for musical training. Simultaneously **Universities** were being established in Paris,

Bologna and Oxford. Musical degrees were being offered. Towns developed as cultural and social centers.

The "**Ars Antiqua**" or "**Old Art**" established with Notre Dame as the central, dominant school of the art.

Cantilena, Clausulae, Conductus, and **Organum** began to fade from significance, replaced by the **Motet** and other new forms.

Melismatic organum (very florid passages) developed with the **Tenor** carrying the plainchant while the other parts are very active. **Isorhythms** developed. Isorhythms are complex rhythmic structures where each voice has its own rhythmic identity. Often, many languages were sung at the same time.

Troubadours sang songs of service, mourning, the dawn, canse, vers and dances in South France.

Trouveres sang chanson, frotaouenge, virelai and ballades in North France.

Minnesingers sang songs in Germany. Spain witnessed monophonic songs including a large number of cantigas and hymns.

Minstrels sang secular songs in England.

1300 A.D

The Ars Nova developed improvisation, duple meter, polyphonic masses, secular music, cannons, hockets, Madrigals and triads (with their sense of chord progression).

There were new forms developed by this time and these forms included the Round, Rondeau, Rota, Rondel, Catch, Chace, Caccia.

The **Motet** served as the foundation for newly composed upper voices usually with two or three voices (the plainchant still provided material for much of the music composed well into the late Middle Ages).

Study: - *Guilliame de Machaut – Quant En Moy*

Composers of the Medieval Age

France – Guillaume de Machaut and **Philippe de Vitry** were very influential in the development of the musical style.

Italy – Jacopo de Bologna and **Landino** were the pioneers to develop the Caccia and the Ballata.

Francis Bacon and **John Wycliffe** were influential thinkers who argued for simplicity in music.

Instruments of the Medieval Age

Psalters

Harp

Viols

Lute

Chimes

Cymbals

Horns

Reeds

Fidel

Portative & Positive Organ.

Renaissance 1400 A.D – 1600 A.D

Introduction

The Renaissance period dates from 1400–1600 A.D. The word **Renaissance means Rebirth**. The Renaissance can be divided into three phases the Early, High, and Late Renaissance.

The return to simplicity, the development of the true vertical harmonic progression, and the introduction of new instruments were some of the characteristics of the Renaissance period. For the first time in history, the idea of perspective was being introduced into art.

Music in the Renaissance

Many new genres were introduced, official **patronage** of the musical arts began. **Secular music** started to gain importance, as most composers were a part of the church, but would also compose music for various occasions and needs . During the Renaissance era, instrumental music was written according to specific rules.

Improvisation was very important in performance and for melodic ornamentation. Transcriptions of vocal music for instrumental performances were numerous. Composers now used instruments liberally in the performance of vocal music. Forms in instrumental music were borrowed from vocal forms, while others were instrumentally invented. Instrumental music also had specific characteristics during the Renaissance Era.

The instrumental style of the Renaissance time period was also distinct.

Melodic range was wider than vocal limitations. The High Middle Ages led to extensive ornamentation which included aspects such as coloration, embellishment, and figuration.

There was a much freer treatment of dissonance. **Contrapuntal** parts were freely added or dropped without indicating rests, in the music involving instruments such as the Lute or most Keyboard adaptations.

There were exceedingly long and rapid scale passages as well as numerous wide skips.

Characteristics of Renaissance Music

Rhythm – A piece in the Renaissance music had various meters; the idea of fixed rhythm was yet to be developed until the Baroque era. The music often had a very slow pace and Meter was introduced during this era. Melody was an important aspect to the music, to give a feel of a poem or a story. Change in dynamics was still largely vocal as instruments were still not able to provide a wide range of volume.

Texture – Polyphonic texture was used widely.

Words and Music – the **Madrigal** was the most important secular genre of the era. Words played an important role and music was set to match the meaning of the word. **Word Painting,** the attempt to express the meaning of words through sound, was developed at this time.

Genres of the Renaissance

Faux Bourdon–a form in which two voices are notated but a third is also sung forming sixths and octaves below.

Madrigals – a secular composition which projected word-painting as the main feature and music was set to compliment the lyrics. Also, the last genre in expressive music before the Opera was introduced. The special feature was the free mix of polyphony and homophony.

Study: - *Jacques Arcadelt - Il Bianco e Dolce Cigno.*

Mass – The Renaissance Mass was largely the most important genre of the Renaissance era. The High Mass (Messa Solemnis) which was roughly introduced during the 7th century, gradually worked its way up also to the Renaissance era.

The Mass varied from seventeen to twenty parts, and could be roughly divided into two main parts.

- The Introduction
- The Eucharist

The **Proper** changed according to the season: The Proper consists of 11 parts of the 17.

The **Ordinary** does not change and consists of Sanctus, Gloria, Kyrie, Credo, Eucharist, Agnus Dei, and Eta-missa-est.

Study: - *Giovanni Pierluigi da Palestrina – Missa Papae Marcelli*

Church Music

Most Renaissance church music was choral **polyphony**, typically sung acappella (without instruments). The main forms were the **mass** and the **motet**. **Chorales** (Protestant hymns) were an important form. Most compositions had four parts, usually based on modes.

Study: - *Giovanni Pierluigi da Palestrina – Viri Galilaei*

One of the most noticeable differences between Medieval and Renaissance styles was that of musical texture and the development of formal polyphony. The key device used to weave this kind of texture is called imitation. Composers were becoming more interested and aware of harmony (how notes fit against each other).

Secular Music

Music independent of churches (i.e., none religious). The most common was the song, which went by various names: lied (German), frottola (Italian), chanson (French), madrigal (Italian), and villancico (Spanish).

Elizabethan Madrigals

A collection of Italian Madrigals with English words was published in England in 1588, and it sparked an interest in English Madrigal writing. They were performed in rich people's homes. There are three kinds of madrigals:

The Madrigal Proper – Is 'through-composed' (The music is different all the time.) There is a lot of word-painting, where music illustrates the meaning of the words. E.g., Thomas Weelkes 'As Vesta was from Latmos Hill descending.'

The Ballett – was also danced sometimes along with singing. The texture is mainly chordal. A madrigal proper is through-composed, whereas a ballett is strophic (two or more verses set to the same music). The most noticeable feature of a ballett is the 'fa-la-la' refrain

The Ayre - An Ayre was performed in a variety of ways: by solo voice with lute accompaniment; by a solo voice with other accompaniment (e.g., viols); all the parts sung by voices (with or without instruments).

Study: - *Matthias Thienel – Myfanwy's Virginal Book*

16th Century Venice

The late 16th century saw the rise of Polychoral (more than one choir) music. The Basilica San Marco di Venezia also known as the Venetian school was the hub to proliferate this movement. Adrian Willaert was the composer, who initiated this style, as a means to solve the problem of delayed singing, caused due to the distances in the chapel. Composers such as Giovanni Gabrielli, who was the principal organist alongside the renowned Gioseffo Zarlino ,who was the maestro di cappella contributed to the movement. This style of singing involved choirs to be pitted against each other, usually from opposing lofts singing antiphonally, involving successive contrasting phrases. The choirs were termed *"cori spezzati"*.

Instrumental Music

Until the beginning of the 16th Century, instruments were less important than voices. They were used for dances, and to accompany vocal music - but here they only doubled the voices. During the 16th Century, however, composers took a greater interest in writing music for instruments. Most of these instruments were intended for outside.

Some examples:

- Lute
- Viol
- Crumhorn

- Rackett
- Sackbut (Early trombone)
- Trumpet (Valveless) English Consorts

A consort is a group of instruments playing together. A whole consort consisted of instruments all from the same family, but a broken consort has instruments from more than one family.

Variations and the Ground Bass

A ground is a tune repeated over and over in the bass, with musical material changing above. Variations are alterations in the tune. There can be variations in the bass as well.

Elizabethan Keyboard Music

The virginal was a popular instrument, and a famous collection was the **'Fitzwilliam Virginal Book'**, which contained over 300 pieces for the virginal. A lot of the music was programmatic (It tells a story, it is descriptive), e.g. 'The King's Hunt', by John Bull.

The Main Characteristics of Renaissance Music are:

1. Music is still based on modes, but gradually more accidentals creep in.
2. Richer texture in four or more parts. Bass part is added below the tenor.
3. Blending rather than contrasting strands in the musical texture.
4. Harmony - Greater concern with the flow and progression of chords.
5. Church music - Some pieces were intended for **'a cappella'** performance. Mainly contrapuntal. Lots of imitation. Church music was now accompanied by instruments - for example polychoral pieces in antiphonal style (Antiphonal Questions and Answers, Stereo Effect).

6. Secular music - (non-religious music. Music in the church was known to be sacred music.) There were many vocal pieces and dances, and an inexhaustible list of instrumental pieces (However a lot of instrumentals were in a vocal style, but some were better suited to the instruments. Vocal music was by far the most important.)

7. The characteristic timbres of Renaissance musical instruments - many forming families.

One of the biggest revolutions of the Renaissance era was the invention of the movable Johannes Gutenberg Printing Press in the year 1450, this invention revolutionized publications of all kinds, including the mass distribution of music.

The **Bible** was the first document to ever be printed on the press.

Some notable historic happenings without a doubt were also the Protestant Reformation (1517) powered by **Martin Luther**.

The church was beginning to lose control and importance in society. The Cynicism caused by the 100 year war also led to the decline of the Church authority in public life.

Composers of the Renaissance

G.P da Palestrina (1526 - 1594) was an Italian composer also known as the savior of harmony and the Prince of Music.

Josquin des Prez (1440 - 1521) was a very dynamic composer of Church Music who also contributed parody masses.

Clement Janequin (1485 - 1558) was a French Composer and was known for his chansons.

Jan Pieterszoon *Sweelinck* (1562 - 1621) was a Dutch composer and pioneer in composing keyboard music.

Gioseffo Zarlino (1517 - 1590) was an Italian composer and a music theorist.

Andrea Gabrieli (1532 - 1585) was an Italian composer and organist.

William Byrd (1539 - 1623) was an English composer and a master in many forms.

Orlando Gibbons (1583 - 1625) was an English composer, virginalist, and organist.

Orlando de Lassus (1532 - 1594) was a Franco- Flemish composer considered to be the greatest polyphonic composers.

Philippe de Monte (1521 - 1603) was a Flemish composer who was known for his madrigals.

Cristobal de Morales (1500 - 1553) was considered to be the most influential Spanish composers of the Renaissance era.

Antonio Cabezon (1510 - 1566) was a Spanish composer and organist.

Instruments of the Renaissance

The Positive

The Portative Organ

Harpsichord

Clavichord

Lutes

Viols

Trumpets

Trombones

Recorders

Flutes

Reeds

Violin

Percussion Instruments.

♪♪

Baroque Era 1600 A.D – 1750 A.D

Introduction to Baroque Era

The Baroque era refers to the time, dated between **1600** (the composition of the First surviving opera) and **1750** (the death of Johann Sebastian Bach). The word Baroque is derived from the Portuguese word meaning an irregularly shaped pearl. The Baroque period is divided into three phases:

Early Baroque   (1600 – 1640)

Middle Baroque   (1640 – 1680)

Late Baroque   (1680 –1750)

The polyphonic texture of Renaissance music was now losing its influence among Early Baroque composers and they preferred using homophonic texture. They felt that words could be projected more clearly, by using just one melody with a chordal accompaniment. The middle phase of the Baroque era saw a new musical style spread from Italy to practically every country in Europe. There was a shift in tonality, major and minor scales were now replacing the medieval or church modes (scales that had governed music for centuries). By about 1680, major or minor scales were the tonal basis of most compositions. Another feature of the Middle Baroque phase was the increased importance of instrumental music. Many compositions paid attention to specific instruments, the violin family being the most popular.

The Late Baroque period witnessed instrumental music becoming as important as vocal music for the first time. Many aspects of harmony, including an emphasis on the attraction of the dominant chord to the tonic arose in this period. Early Baroque composers had emphasized homophonic texture; Late Baroque composers took polyphony towards greater heights.

Music in Baroque Society

Before 1600, most music was written in order, to meet specific demands that came mainly from churches and aristocratic courts. Now institutions such as Opera houses and municipalities were also in a constant need for supply of music. Regardless, the demand was for new music, audiences did not want to immerse in listening to pieces in an 'old fashioned style'.

Church music was often very grand. Along with an organ and a choir, many baroque churches had an orchestra to accompany services. Indeed, it was in the church that most ordinary citizens heard music.

Musicians were now employed to play in a variety of functions in larger towns, some of which included playing in churches, in processions, in concert and in university graduations. Some baroque musicians earned money by writing operas for commercial opera houses.

To get a job, musicians usually had to perform and submit compositions. Composers and Musicians were an integral part of the baroque society working for courts, churches, towns and commercial opera houses.

Although they wrote their music to meet specific needs and occasions, the quality they achieved wass so high that much of it has become the standard in most of today's concert repertoire.

Characteristics of Baroque music

1) **Unity of Mood**: - A Baroque piece usually expresses one basic mood, the emotion expressed at the start of the piece will remain throughout until the end. Specific rhythm or melodic patterns were associated with specific moods. "Affections" was a term ascribed to the emotional state in baroque music, they go onto represent different emotional states such as joy, grief, fanfare, pomp and agitation.

2) **Rhythm**: - Unity of mood in Baroque music is conveyed, first of all, by continuity of rhythm. The rhythmic pattern heard at the beginning of a piece would be repeated throughout. This rhythmic continuity provides a compelling drive and energy – the forward motion is rarely interrupted.

3) **Melody**: - Baroque melody also creates a feeling of continuity. An opening melody will be heard again and again in the course of a Baroque piece.

4) **Dynamics**: - When the dynamics did shift it was usually sudden. This alternation between loud and soft is called terraced dynamics. The main keyboard instruments of the Baroque period were the organ and harpsichord, both well suited for continuity of dynamic level.

5) **Texture**: - Homophonic texture was employed exclusively in the operas and in solo arias of all kinds. Polyphonic texture was achieved by tonal counterpoint. It was used in religious chord works as well as in many types of instrumental composition such as the Fugue or variations on a ground bass.

6) **Chords and the Basso Continuo (Figured Bass)**: - Chords became increasingly important during the Baroque period. In earlier times, there was more concern with the beauty of individual melodic lines than with the chords formed when the lines were heard together. The new emphasis on chords and the bass part resulted in the most characteristic feature of Baroque music, an accompaniment called the Basso Continuo or Figured bass. This is made up of a bass part together with numbers, which specify the chords to be played above it.

7) **Words and Music**: - Like their Renaissance predecessors, Baroque composers used music to depict the meaning of specific words. "Heaven" might be set to a high tone and "Hell" to a low tone. Ascending scales represented upward motion; descending scales depicted downward motion. Descending chromatic scales depicted pain, sorrow, loss, and grief. Baroque composers often emphasized words by writing many rapid notes for a single syllable of text; this technique also displayed singer virtuosity.

The Baroque Orchestra

The Baroque Orchestra evolved into a performing group, based on instruments of the violin family. By modern standards, the Baroque orchestra was small, consisting of ten to thirty or forty players. Its instrumental makeup was flexible and could vary from piece to piece.

The basso continuo (harpsichord plus cello, double bass or bassoon) and upper strings (first and second violins and violas) were the core of the Baroque Orchestra. The use of woodwind, brass, and percussion instruments was variable. To the strings and the basso continuo, recorders, flutes, oboes, trumpets, horns, trombones or timpani could be added. One piece might use only a single flute, while another would call for two oboes, three trumpets, and timpani. During festive occasions, instruments such as trumpets and timpani joined the orchestra. This flexibility contrasts with the standardized orchestra of later periods, consisting of four sections- strings, woodwinds, brass, and percussion.

The Baroque trumpet (like Earl French Horn) had no valves but was given rapid, complex melodic lines to play in a high register because the instrument was difficult to play and had a tradition with royalty, the trumpet was the aristocrat of the Baroque orchestra.

Study: - Bach - Orchestral Suite no. 3 in D major BWV 1068

The Concerto Grosso and Ritornello form

The Concerto Grosso is an important form of orchestral music in the late Baroque period. In a Concerto Grosso, a small group of soloists are pitted against a larger group of players called the tutti (all). Usually, two or four soloists play with eight to twenty or more musicians for the tutti. The tutti comprises predominantly of string instruments, with the harpsichord as a part of the basso continuo. A Concerto Grosso presents a contrast of texture between the tutti and the soloist, who assert their individuality and appeal for attention through brilliant and fanciful melodic lines.

A Concerto Grosso characteristically consists of movements, few or multiple that contrast in tempo and character. Most often there are three movements.

    1) Fast

    2) Slow

    3) Fast.

The opening movement is usually vigorous and determined, clearly showing the contrast between tutti and the soloist. The second movement is usually quieter than the first, often lyrical and intimate. The last movement is lively and carefree sometimes dance-like.

The opening and the closing movements of the Concerto Grosso are quite often in Ritornello Form, based on successive trade-offs between the tutti and solo sections. In Ritornello Form, the tutti plays an opening theme which is called the Ritornello. This theme, which has always been played by the tutti, continues to play throughout the movement in different keys but it usually returns in fragments, not complete. Only at the end of the movement does the entire Ritornello return in the home key. While each composition has a different number of Ritornellos (tuttis), a Concerto Grosso movement typically has the following structure.

1. a. Tutti (f), ritornello in home key

    a. Solo

2. a. Tutti (f), ritornello fragment

    a. Solo

3. a. Tutti (f), ritornello fragment

    a. Solo

4. a. Tutti (f), ritornello in home key

In contrast to the tutti's ritornello, the solo section offers fresh melodic ideas, softer dynamics, rapid scales, and broken chords. Additionally, soloists might develop brief melodic ideas from the tutti. The opening movement of Bach's Brandenburg Concert No.5 is a fine example of Ritornello Form in the Concerto Grosso.

Study: - *Arcangelo Corelli (1653-1713): Concerto Grosso in D, Op. 6, no.1*

The Fugue

A Fugue is a polyphonic composition based on one main theme called a "subject". Throughout a Fugue, different melodic lines, or "voices" imitate the subject. The top melodic line whether sung or played is the soprano voice and the bottom is the bass.

The opening of a Fugue in four vices may be represented as follows:

Soprano

Subject……………………………………………….etc

Alto

Subject……………………………………….etc

Tenor

Subject………………………………..etc

Bass

Subject…………………………..etc

A distinct and different melodic concept known as a "Countersubject" frequently accompanies the subject in another voice of a Fugue. The countersubject is always present with the subject, occasionally appearing above or below it.

Before presentation of the subject there are often transitional sections called "episodes", which offer either new material or fragments of the subject or countersubject. "Episodes" do not present the subject in its entirety.

A Fugue is introduced by a short piece called prelude.

Study: - *Organ Fugue in G minor (little fugue, about 1709), by Johan Sebastian Bach.*

The Baroque Opera

The Baroque Opera witnessed the development of a major innovation in Music – "opera", or drama that is sung to orchestral accompaniment.

This unique fusion of music, acting, poetry, dance, scenery and costumes offers a theatrical experience of overwhelming excitement and emotion. Since its beginning in Italy around 1600, opera has spread to many countries and it remains a powerful form of musical theater today.

In an opera, characters and plot are revealed through songs, rather than the speech used in ordinary drama. Opera demands performers who can sing and act simultaneously. Opera may contain spoken dialogue but most are entirely sung. Some operas are serious, some comic, some both. Spoken dialogue is used mainly in comic opera since it normally takes longer to sing than to speak them. .

Some of the voice categories of opera are:

a) Coloratura Soprano – Very high range: can execute rapid scales and trills.

b) Lyric Soprano – Rather light voice; sings notes calling for grace and charm

c) Dramatic Soprano – Full, powerful voice, is capable of passionate intensity

d) Lyric Tenor – Relatively light, bright voice.

e) Dramatic Tenor – Powerful voice, is capable of heroic expression.

f) Basso Buffo – Takes comic roles, can sing very rapidly

g) Basso profound – Very low, powerful voice, takes roles calling for great dignity.

The main attraction for many opera fans is the Aria, a song for solo voice with orchestral accompaniment. It is an outpouring of melody that expresses an emotional state. An Aria usually lasts several minutes. It is a complete piece with a definite beginning high point and end.

Opera composers often lead into an Aria with a recitative, a vocal line that imitates the rhythm and pitch fluctuation of speech. In a recitative (from the Italian word for "recite") words are sung quickly and clearly, often and with repeated tones. There is usually only one note to each syllable in a recitative – as opposed to an Aria, where one syllable may be stretched over many notes.

Beside Arias, the soloist in an opera will sing compositions of two or more singers, duet (for two singer), trios (for three), quartets (for four), quintets (for five) and sextets (for six). An ensemble is a composition that includes three or more vocalists. An overture or prelude is a purely orchestral piece that typically opens an opera.

Study: - Claudio Monteverdi - L`Orfeo

The Chorale and Church Cantata

The Chorale: - In Leipzig in Bach's time, the Lutheran Church service on Sunday was the social event of the week: it started at seven in the morning and lasted about 4 hours. The sermon alone would take an hour.

An important component of the Lutheran service was music. The service was filled with music, a single composition might last half an hour.

Each service included several hymns or Chorales.

The Chorale or hymn tune was sung to a German religious text, Chorales were easy to sing and remember, having only one note to a syllable and moving in steady rhythm. They were tunes that had been composed in the sixteenth and seventeenth centuries or had been adopted from folk songs and Catholic hymns.

The Church Cantata: - Cantata originally meant a piece that was sung as opposed to a Sonata, which was played. Many kinds of Cantatas were being written in Bach's day, one of them was the Cantata designed for the Lutheran service in Germany in the early 1700s. It was usually written for chorus, vocal soloist, organ and a small orchestra. It contained a religious passage in German, either freshly composed or taken from well- known songs or the Bible.

Bach wrote about 395; about 195 are still in existence.

Study: - Bach - Cantata Weichet nur, betrübte Schatten BWV 202

The Oratorio:

The Oratorio, together with the opera and the cantata, represents a significant advancement in baroque vocal music. Like an opera, the Oratorio is a large – scale composition for chorus, vocal soloist and orchestra, it is usually set to a narrative text. Opera is different from the Oratorio, in that the former lacks actors, sets, and costumes. Most Oratorios are based on biblical stories, but usually they are not intended for religious services.

A series of choruses, arias, duets, recitatives, and orchestral interludes make up an Oratorio. The chorus has a particularly significant role in the drama, offering commentary or engaging in it themselves. Recitatives by narrators typically narrate the tale and make connections between different parts. Oratories are longer than Cantatas (more than 2 hours sometimes) and have more of a story line.

Oratories first appeared in early 17th century. These days, churches or music halls host their performances.

Messiah by George Frideric Handel, has for decades been the best known and most loved Oratorio.

Study: - *George Frederic Handel – Messiah*

Composers of the Baroque Era

Claudio Monteverdi	(1567 - 1643)
Jean-Baptiste Lully	(1632 - 1687)
Dieterich Buxtehude	(1637 - 1707)
Johann Pachelbel	(1653 - 1706)
Arcangelo Corelli	(1653 - 1713)
Henry Purcell	(1659 - 1695)
Antonio Vivaldi	(1678 - 1741)

Georg Philipp Telemann	(1681 - 1767)
Jean-Philippe Rameau	(1683 - 1764)
Johann Sebastian Bach	(1685 - 1750)
George Frideric Handel	(1685 - 1759)
Domenico Scarlatti	(1685 - 1757)
Giovanni Battista Pergolesi	(1710 - 1736)

The Classical Era 1750 A.D – 1827 A.D

Introduction to the Classical Era

The classical era refers to the time dated between **1750** (Death of Bach) and **1827** (Death of Ludwig Van Beethoven). Since the word "classical" refers to various things, therefore it might be confusing. It may refer to Greek or Roman antiquity, or it may be used for any supreme accomplishment of lasting appeal (as in the expression movie classic). Many people take classical music to be something that is not rock, jazz, folk or popular music. Music historians have borrowed the term "classical" referring to the works of those 18th -century composers.

In music history, the time roughly spanning from 1730 to 1770 is referred to as the "pre classical" period; it marks the change from the Baroque style to the full blooming of the classical. It was evolving concurrently with the Baroque masterworks of Bach and Handel.

Around the middle of the 18th century, composers concentrated on simplicity and clarity, discarding much that had enriched late Baroque music. Polyphonic texture was neglected in favor of tuneful melody and single harmony. Composers began to write music offering contrasts of mood and theme.

Music in Classical Era Society

Music in the classical era served a highly sophisticated and aristocratic society. Its most common function was to provide delightful entertainment for guests. Music also served to be an important function in the home, for this was an Era of amateur musical performances, both vocal and instrumental. Many serious composers were called upon to write Chamber music, as well as vocal solos and ensembles for amateur consumption. Naturally, music for dancing was in popular demand for a society that loved gaiety and entertainment. While the church was not a major consumer of serious music, it still demanded that composers write sacred music for services in the spirit of secularism that prevailed then.

As the 18th century advanced, people made more money. There was a rapid growth in the middle-class society and in fact, during the classical period, the middle-class had a great influence on music, because palace concerts were usually closed to them, towns' people organized public concerts. Composers in the classical period took middle class tastes into account and wrote especially for the middle-class audiences.

Characteristic of the Classical Style

1) **Contrast of mood:** - While a late Baroque piece may convey a single emotion, a classical composition would fluctuate the mood. A carefree dance tune could follow a dramatic, stormy piece of music. Mood in classical music would change gradually or suddenly however the classical composer firmly controls such conflicts and contrast.

2) **Rhythm:** - Flexibility of rhythm adds to variety in classical music. A classical composition has a wealth of rhythmic patterns, whereas a Baroque piece contains a few patterns that are reiterated throughout. One can fairly and accurately predict the rhythmic pattern of a whole movement, after opening the few bars of baroque pieces, which give a sense of continuity and eternal motion but classical style includes unexpected pauses, syncopations and frequent changes from long notes to shorter notes.

3) **Texture:** - In contrast to the polyphonic texture of late Baroque music, classical music is basically homophonic. However, texture is treated as flexibly, as rhythm. Pieces change textures either gradually or abruptly. A piece of music can start out homophonically with a melody and straight forward accompaniment before switching to a more intricate polyphonic texture, with two melodies playing at one time or parts of melody that are reproduced among the various instruments.

4) **Melody:** - Classical melodies are among the most tuneful and easiest to remember. The themes of even highly sophisticated

composition may have a folk or popular flavor. Because classical melodies usually consist of two phrases that have the same duration, they generally sound balanced and symmetrical, however Baroque melodies, on the contrary tend to be less symmetrical, more elaborate and harder to sing

5) **Dynamics and the piano:** - Classical composers' interest in expressing shades of emotion led to a widespread use of gradual dynamic change - crescendo and decrescendo. Crescendo and Decrescendos were an electrifying novelty; audiences sometimes rose excitedly from their seats.

During the classical period, the desire for gradual dynamic change led to the replacement of the harpsichord by the piano. By varying the finer pressure on the keys, a pianist could play more loudly or softly.

Although the first pianos were built around 1709 by Bartolomeo Cristofori in Florence, Italy. It began to replace the harpsichord only around 1775. Most of the mature keyboard compositions of Haydn, Mozart and Beethoven were written for piano, rather than harpsichord, clavichord and organ.

The Classical orchestra

A new orchestra evolved during the classical period. Unlike Baroque orchestra, which could vary from piece to piece, it was a standard group of four sections - strings, woodwinds, brass and percussion.

The number of musicians were greater in a classical orchestra than in a Baroque group. A classical orchestral piece has greater variety and a rapid changes of tone.. A theme might begin in the full orchestra, shift to the strings and then continue in the woodwinds. Unlike Baroque Orchestra composers, they did not treat instruments like another voice. The violin melody would never be repeated by an oboe, throughout the whole movement by classical composers.

The classical orchestra had several sections and each had a distinct function. The strings were the most important section, with the first violins taking the melody, most of the time and the lower strings providing an accompaniment. The woodwinds added contrasting tone colors and were given melodic solos. Horns and trumpets brought power to loud passages and filled out the harmony, but they did not usually play the main melody. The timpani were used for rhythmic bite and emphasis. On the whole, the classical orchestra had developed into a flexible, colorful instrument in which composers could entrust their most powerful and dramatic musical conception.

Vienna

Vienna was one of the music centers of Europe, during the classical period and Haydn, Mozart and Beethoven were all active there. Its population of almost 250,000 (in 1810) made Vienna the fourth largest city in Europe. All the three classical masters mentioned above were born elsewhere, but they were drawn to Vienna to study and to seek recognition.

The classical style reached its zenith between about 1770-1789 in Vienna and was consequently called the Viennese classical style. The classical style developed in and around Vienna for several reasons. Vienna stood at the crossroads of four very musical nations, Germany (both protestant north and Catholic south), Italy, Bohemia and Hungary. Vienna was home to rich and powerful aristocrats and a well-off middle class, all of whom were music enthusiasts.

Theme and Variations

The form called theme and variation was widely used in the classical period, either as an independent piece or as one movement of a symphony, sonata, or string quartet. In a theme and variations, a basic musical idea – the theme – repeats and is changed each time. This form may be outlined as theme (A) – variation 1 (A') – variation 2 (A") – Variation 3 (A''') and so on; each prime mark indicates a variation of the basic idea.

Each variation, though usually about the same length as the theme, is unique and may differ in mood from the theme. A variation can be given its unique identity by adjusting the dynamics, melody, rhythm, harmony, accompaniment, tone colour, and/or accompaniment. The main melody might repeat in a minor key rather than a major key, or it might emerge in the bass. It might be heard next to a brand-new melody.

Study: *Ah vous dirai – je, maman (Wolfgang Amadeus Mozart)*

Minuet and Trio

The third movement in classical symphonies, **string quartets,** and other works is in the form known as minuet and trio or **minuet.** The minuet originated as a dance and it first appeared at the court of Louis XIV of France around 1650 and was danced by aristocrats throughout the 18th century.

The minuet movement of a symphony or string quartet is written for listening not for dancing. While the tempo is moderate, the time signature is in triple meter. The movement is in A B A form: minuet (A), trio (B), minuet (A). The trio (B) is usually quieter than the minuet (A) section and requires fewer instruments. It usually contains woodwind solos.

Section A (miniature) contains smaller **sections** a, b and **a' (variant** of a). In the opening A (minuet) section, all the smaller parts are repeated as follows: a (repeated) b a'(repeated). The B (trio) section is quite similar in form: C (repeated) d c' (repeated). At the close of the B (trio) section, the entire A(minuet) section is repeated again.

Minuet Trio

A B

A (repeated) b a' (repeated) C (repeated) d c' (repeated)

Minuet A

a b a'

Study: – EineKleineNachtmusik, K 525, (Wolfgang Amadeus Mozart)

Rhondo

Many classical movements are in Rondo form. The main theme **(a)** is composed in a Circle that returns several times **alternating** with other themes. Common Rhondo patterns are ABACA and ABACABA. The main theme is usually lively, pleasing and simple to remember and the listener can easily recognize its return because the main theme usually started in the tonic key.

Study: - String Quartet in C minor, op.18, no. 4, Ludwig Van Beethoven

Sonata Form

An astonishing amount of important music from the classical period to the 20th century is composed in Sonata form (sometimes called sonata allegro). The term Sonata form refers to the form of a single movement. It should not be confused with the term Sonata, which is used for a whole composition made up of several movements.

A Sonata-Form movement consists of three main sections, the **exposition**, where the themes are presented, the **development**, where themes are treated in new ways and the **recapitulation**, where the themes return. Then followed by a concluding section, the **coda** (Italian for tail). Remember that these sections are all within one movement.

Exposition
- a) First theme in tonic (home) key.
- b) Bridge containing modulation from home key to new key.
- c) Second theme in new key.
- d) Closing section in key of second theme.

Development
- a) New treatment of themes; modulation to different keys.

Recapitulation
- **a)** First theme in tonic key.
- **b)** Bridge.
- **c)** Second theme in tonic key.
- **d)** Closing section in tonic key.

Coda
- **a)** In tonic key.

Study: - Symphony no.40 in G minor, K 550 (Wolfgang Amadeus Mozart)

Composers of the Classical Era

Wolfgang Amadeus Mozart	1756 - 1791
Franz Joseph Haydn	1732 - 1809
Ludwig van Beethoven	1770 - 1827
Franz Schubert	1797 - 1828
Carl Philipp Emanuel Bach	1714 - 1788
Luigi Boccherini	1743 - 1805

Romantic Era 1827 A.D – 1900 A.D

Introduction to the Romantic Era

The Romantic Era refers to the time dated between 1827 (death of Ludwig Van Beethoven) and 1900. It is difficult to draw absolute distinction between Classical and Romantic era music. The Romantic era of the 19th century saw an intensification and extension of the expressive elements of classicism, but did not mark a musical stylistic break with classicism. Some composers of the Romantic Era used them extensively and some used them contextually. Some abandoned them altogether, replacing them with new form that included compositional miniatures.

Nonetheless, there are many differences between Romantic and Classical music. Romantic works tend to have greater range of tone color, dynamics and pitch. Additionally, the array of chord progressions and vocabulary in the Romantic era is more extensive, accentuating bright, unsteady harmonies. Romantic music has a stronger connection to the other arts, especially literature.

Music in Romantic Era Society

The composer's purview and disposition in general changed drastically during Beethoven's lifetime (1770-1827). In earlier periods, part of a musician's job had been to compose works for a specific occasion and audience, but romantic composers were not only interested in pleasing their contemporaries but also in being judged favorably by posterity..

Sometimes the romantic composer was a "free artist" by necessity rather than choice, because of the French revolution and Napoleon wars (from 1789 to 1815), many aristocrats could no longer afford to maintain private opera houses, orchestras and "composers in residence."

However, during the 19th century, cities expanded dramatically and a sizeable number of people wanted to hear and play music. The first half of the 19th century also witnessed the founding of music conservatories throughout Europe. More young men and women than ever before studied to be professional musicians. At first women were accepted only as a student of performance, but by the late 1800s, they could study musical compositions as well.

The 19th century public was captivated by virtuosity. Among the musical heroes of the 1830s were the pianist Franz Liszt and the violinist Nicolo Paganini (2782 -1840), who toured Europe and astonished audiences with their feats.

Private music making also increased during the Romantic era. The piano became a fixture in every middle- class home and there was a great demand for songs and solo piano pieces.

Characteristics of Romantic Music

1) **Individuality of style:** - Romantic music puts unprecedented emphasis on self- expression and individuality of style. Numerous composers in the Romantic era made music that sounded extraordinary and mirrored their characters.

2) **Expressive Aims and Subjects**: - The romantic explored a universe of feeling that included flamboyance and intimacy, unpredictability and melancholy, rapture and longing, countless songs and operas glorifying romantic love. More often than not, the lovers are troubled and face overpowering obstructions. Interest in the extraordinary and infernal was communicated in music. All aspects of nature attracted romantic musicians. Romantic composers also dealt with subjects drawn from the middle- ages and Shakespeare's plays.

3) **Expressive Tone color:** - Romantic composers reveled in rich and sensuous sound, using tone color to obtain variety of mood and atmosphere. Never before had timbre been so important.

4) **Colorful Harmony:** - In addition to exploiting new tone colors, the romantics' explored new chords and novel ways of using familiar chords. Seeking greater emotional intensity, composers emphasized

rich, colorful and complex harmonies. There was a prominent use of chromatic harmony, which uses chords containing tones, not found in the prevailing major or minor scales. Chromatic chords add color and motion to romantic music. Unstable, dissonant harmonies were more openly used, than during the old-style period. A piece in the Romantic era had a wide heterogeneity of keys and quick balances, or changes starting with one critical and then onto the next. Towards the end of the Romantic period, much more accentuation was given to harmonic ambiguity and less to a robust stable progression and resolution.

5) **Expanded range of Dynamics, Pitch, and Tempo**: - Romantic music also calls for a wide range of dynamics. It includes sharp contrasts between faint whispers and sonorities with unprecedented power. The classical dynamics extremes – ff and pp didn't meet the needs of romantics, who sometimes demanded *ffff* and *ppppp*. Seeking more and more expressiveness, 19th century composers used frequent crescendos and decrescendos, as well as sudden dynamic changes.

The range of pitch was expanded too, as composers reached for extremely high or low sounds the romantics used instruments like the piccolo, contrabassoon, and piano. They expanded keyboard to achieve greater brilliance and depth of sound.

Changes of mood in romantic music are often underlined by accelerando, ritardando and subtle variations of pace, there are many more fluctuations in tempo than, there are in classical music. To intensify the expression of music, romantic performers made use of the rubato, a slight holding back or pressing forward of tempo.

6) **Forms Miniature and Monumental:** - Romantic composers characteristically expressed themselves both in musical miniatures and in monumental compositions. On the other hand, there are piano pieces by Chopin and songs by Schubert that last but a few minutes. Such short forms were meant to be heard in the intimate surroundings of a home; they met the needs of the growing number of people who owned a piano. On the other hand, there are gigantic works by Berlioz and Wagner that call for a huge number of performers, that last for several hours and were designed for large opera houses or concert halls.

The Art song and the song cycle

One of the most distinctive form in Romantic music is the art song, a composition for solo voice and piano. Here, the accompaniment is an integral part of the composer's conception and it serves as an interpretive partner to the voice.

Music and poetry are personally combined in the art song. It is no mishap that this structure bloomed with the development, of a rich collection of Romantic poetry in the mid-nineteenth century. Song composers would interpret a poem, translating its mood, atmosphere and imagery into music. They created a vocal melody that was musically satisfying and perfectly molded to the text. Significant words were underscored by focused tones or melodic peaks. The voice imparts the interpretive commission to the piano.

Emotions and image of the text take on added dimension from the keyboard commentary. Arpeggios in the piano could propose the sprinkling of paddles or the movement of a factory wheel. Chords in a low register might depict darkness or a lover's torment. A brief piano introduction set the mood, summed up at the end by a piano section called a 'postlude."

The song cycle: - Romantic art songs are sometimes grouped in a set or "song cycle". A cycle might be brought together by a storyline, that goes through the sonnets, or melodic motifs connecting the tunes.

In many of their art songs, romantic composers achieved a perfect union of music and poetry. Among the great songs cycles are "Die winterreise" (The winter Journey, 1827) by Schubert and Dichter Liebe (poet's love, 1840) by Robert Schumann.

Program music

The 19th century was the great age of program music, instrumental music associated with a story, poem idea or scene. A programmatic instrumental piece can represent the emotions, characters and events of a particular story, or it can evolve the sounds and motion of nature. Program music in some form or another has existed for centuries, but it became particularly prominent in the Romantic period, when music was closely associated with literature.

Study: *- (Fantastic Symphony, 1830)*

Nationalism and exoticism

Nationalism was a significant political development that affected 19th century music. Musical nationalism was expressed when romantic composers deliberately created music with a specific national identity, using the folk songs, dances, legends and history of their homeland. Fascination with national identity also led composers to draw on colorful materials from foreign lands, a trend known as musical "exoticism". For instance, some composers wrote melodies in an Asian style or used rhythm and instruments associated with distant lands. For instance, Italian composer, Giacomo Puccini evoked Japan in his opera Madame Butterfly.

Study: *- The Moldau (1874) by Bedrich Smetana*

Composers of the Romantic

Era Frédéric Chopin	1810 - 1849
Franz Liszt	1811 - 1886
Johannes Brahms	1833 - 1897
Richard Wagner	1813 - 1883
Pyotr Ilyich Tchaikovsky	1840 - 1893
Giuseppe Verdi	1813 - 1901
Gustav Mahler	1860 - 1911
Robert Schumann	1810 - 1856
Bedřich Smetana	1824 - 1884

The Twentieth Century Modern Era 1900 A.D – 1990 A.D

Introduction To the Twentieth Century

In music, as in the other arts, the early 20th century was a time of revolt. The years following, 1900 saw fundamental changes in the language of music, than any other time since the beginning of the Baroque Era. There were entirely new approaches to the organization of pitch and rhythm and a vast expansion in the vocabulary of sounds, especially percussion sounds.

From the late 1600s to about 1900, musical structure was governed by certain general principles, however since 1900, no single system has governed the organization of pitch in all musical compositions. Each piece is bound to have an extraordinary arrangement of pitch connections.

In the past, composers depended on the listener's awareness – conscious or unconscious – of the general principles underlying the interrelationship of tones and chords. For example, they relied on the listener's expectations that a dominant chord would follow a tonic. By substituting another chord for the expected one, a composer could create a feeling of suspense, drama or surprise, but 20th – century music relies less on pre-established relationships and expectations. This new approach to the organizations of sound makes 20th – century music fascinating.

Musical innovations since 1945 have been more far reaching than those of the first half of the 20th – century. There have been many new directions, and range of musical styles and the system is wider than ever.

Characteristic Of Twentieth Century Music

1. Tone Color

During the 20th century, tone color became a more important element of music than it ever was before. It often took a major role, creating variety, continuity, and mood. In the music of the modern era, clamor-like and percussive sounds are frequently utilized, and instruments are played at the extremely top or lower part of their ranges. Uncommon playing techniques have become normal. For example, the glissando, a rapid slide up and down a scale, is more widely used.

Woodwind and brass players are often asked to produce a fluttery sound by rapidly rolling the tongue while playing. And string players frequently strike the string with the stick of the bow, rather than draw the bow across the strings.

Percussion instruments have become prominent and numerous, reflecting the 20th century interest in unusual rhythms and tone colors. Instruments that became standard during the 1900's include the xylophone, celesta, and woodblock, to name a few.

Composer's occasionally call for noise makers - typewriters, sirens, automobile brake drums.

2. Harmony Consonance and dissonance

The 20th century established foundational changes and impacted the means of how harmonies are dealt with.

Up to about 1900, chords were divided into two opposite types: consonant and dissonant. A consonant chord was stable; it functioned as a point of rest or arrival. A dissonant chord was unstable; its tension demanded onward motion, or resolution to a stable consonant chord. Traditionally, only the triad, a three- tone chord could be consonant. All the other were considered dissonant. In the 19th century, composers came to use ever more dissonant chords, and they treated dissonance with increasing freedom. By the mid- 20th century, the conventional differentiation among consonance and cacophony (dissonance) was deserted in much music.

New chord structures

Before 1900, there were general principles governing chord construction: certain combinations of tones were considered chords, while others were not. At the core of traditional harmony is the triads, although the triad often appears in 20th century music, it is no longer so fundamental. Some 20th century composers created fresh harmonies by placing one traditional chord against another. Such a combination of two chords heard at the same time is called *polychord*. A paradigm shift in 20th-century music was the utilization of chordal designs of which triads were not the base.

One such commonly used is the *fourth chord*, in which the tones are a fourth apart, instead of a third.

Alternatives to the traditional tonal system. In addition to creating new chord structures, 20th century composers explored alternatives to the traditional tonal system. After 1900 some composers continued to use the traditional system, but others modified it greatly and still others discarded it entirely.

To create fresh sounds, composers used scales other than major or minor. For example, they breathed new life into the church modes-scales that had been used before 1600 as well as in folk songs of every period. Other scales were borrowed from the musical traditions of lands outside Western Europe, and still others were invented by composers.

3. Rhythm

The new techniques of organizing pitch were accompanied by new means of organizing rhythm. Music's rhythmic vocabulary was expanded, with an increased emphasis on unpredictability and irregularity. Rhythm was one of the most striking components of 20th-century music; where it indicated power, drive, and energy. Rapidly changing meters are characteristic of 20th century music, whereas Baroque, Classical, and Romantic music, maintain a single meter throughout a movement or section.

20th-century music often has two or more contrasting independent rhythms at the same time; this is called *polyrhythm*. Each part of the musical texture goes its own rhythmic way, often creating accents that are out of phase with accents in the other part. Different meters are used at the same time. For example, one instrument may play in duple meter (1-2, 1-2) while another plays in triple meter (1-2-3, 1-2-3). The polyrhythm of jazz strongly influenced composers in the 1920's and 1930's.

4. Melody

The new technique of pitch and rhythmic organization, that we have surveyed, had strong impact on 20th century melody. Melody was no longer necessarily associated with major and minor keys or conventional chord progressions. It could be based to a wide variety of scales, or it could freely use all twelve chromatic tones and have no tonal center. Melody today often contains wide leaps that are difficult to sing. Rhythmic irregularity and changing meters tend to make 20th century melodies unpredictable.

MUSIC IN MODERN ERA SOCIETY

The 20th century has seen dramatic changes in how music reaches its listeners. The living room became the new "concert hall" through recordings, radio and television. This technological advance brought music to a larger audience than ever before, besides vastly increasing the range of music available. Radio broadcasts of live or recorded music began to reach a larger audience during the 1920's.

In the 1930's radio networks in several countries formed orchestras specifically to perform live music. With television broadcast, music performances could be seen as well as heard. During the start of the 1950's major orchestras and opera companies began to programme 20th century music. Long playing recordings gave listeners access to works, that had seemed incomprehensible; these works could now be played repeatedly until they were understood and enjoyed.

Ballad and opera companies, foundations, orchestra, performers, film studios, and wealthy music lovers commissioned modern compositions. Developments in dance had an especially strong impact on 20th- century music. Films provided a new stimulus for music too, and most film scores were background music. Most composers were and still are also teachers, conductors, or performers. Some have become composers in residence with symphony orchestras. They advised music directors on the contemporary repertoire and composed work for performance, by the host orchestra.

In the 20th century more women than ever before, became active as composers, virtuoso soloists and music educators. African - American composers and performers - both women and men – had become increasingly prominent in the 20th century. For many years African-American musicians were admitted in music schools but were barred as performers and conductors in established orchestra companies and symphony orchestras. During the 20th-century, the US turned into an influential entity in music. American jazz and popular music swept the world. And since the 1950's, many universities have sponsored performing groups specializing in 20th century music. In addition, they have housed most of the electronic music studios.

Neoclassicism

From about 1920 to 1950, the music of many composers, including Igor Stravinsky and Paul Hindemith, reflected an artistic movement known as Neoclassicism. Neoclassicism is marked by emotional restrain, balance, and clarity; Neoclassic compositions use musical forms and stylistic features of earlier period, particularly of the 18th century. Neo classicism composers turned away from programmed music and then the gigantic orchestra favored at the turn of the century. They preferred absolute (non-programmatic) music for chamber groups. Neoclassic music is not merely a revival of all forms and styles; it uses earlier techniques to organize 20th century harmonies and rhythms.

Expressionism

Much of the music of the 20th century reflects an artistic movement called Expressionism, which stressed on intense, subjective emotions. It was, to a great extent, focused in Germany and Austria from 1905-1925. Expressionism outgrew similar scholarly environment as Freud's investigations of delirium and the oblivious. 20th- century musical Expressionism grows out of the emotional turbulence in the works of the late Romantics like Wagner, Richard Strauss, and Mahler.

Musical style since 1945 (Jazz, The American Musical, Rock)

Jazz

About the time Schoenberg and Stravinsky were changing the language of Europe, a new music style was being developed in the United States. It was created by musicians predominantly African - Americans performing in streets, bars, and dance halls of New Orleans and other southern cities. Jazz can be described generally as music rooted in improvisation and characteristics of syncopated rhythm, a steady beat, and distinctive tone color as a performance technique.

Although jazz became current in 1917, the music itself was probably heard as early as 1900. We don't have the foggiest idea when jazz began or how it sounded from the outset, since this new music existed exclusively in execution, not in melodic documentation. Since its beginning, jazz has developed a rich variety of sub-styles such as New Orleans style (or Dixie land), Swing, Bebop, Cool, Free Jazz and Jazz Rock. It has produced such outstanding figures as Louis Armstrong, Duke Ellington, Benny Goodman, Charlie Barker and Miles Davis.

The American musical

A musical or musical comedy is a type of theater that fuses script, acting and spoken dialect with music, singing, and dancing with scenery, costumes, and spectacle. Most musicals are in fact comedies, though some are serious. Generally, a musical is in two acts of which the second is shorter and brings back some of the melodies heard earlier. Traditionally, the song consisted of an introductory section (the verse) and a main section (the chorus) in AABA form (32 bars). Hit songs like *Ol' Man River* (from showboat) and *Some Enchanted Evening* (from south pacific) often has lasting appeal, independent of the theatrical context.

In contrast to opera, it tends to use simpler harmonies, melodies, and structures; it has more spoken dialects; and its songs have a narrower pitch range. Also, the musical is an even more collaborative effort: one composer may create a song, and other musicians are responsible for orchestration, the overture, connective musical passage, and ballads. The book and the lyrics are usually written by several people.

Rock

The mid 1950's saw the growth of a new kind of popular music that was first called *rock and roll* and then simply *rock*. Though it includes diverse styles, *rock* tends to be vocal music with a hard, driving beat, often featuring electric guitar accompaniment and heavily amplified sound.

Early *rock* grew mainly out of *rhythm and blues,* a dance music of African American origin that fused blues, jazz, and gospel styles. *Rock* also drew upon *country and western*, a folk like, and guitar- based style associated with rural white Americans. In little more than a decade, **rock** evolved from a simple dance- oriented style to music that was highly varied in its tone colors, lyrics and electronic technology.

Composers of the Modern Era

Igor Stravinsky	(1882 - 1971)
Arnold Schoenberg	(1874 - 1951)
Sergei Prokodiev	(1891 - 1953)
Aaron Copland	(1900 - 1990)
Dmitri Shostakovich	(1906 - 1975)
Maurice Ravel	(1875 - 1937)
George Gershwin	(1898 - 1937)
Claude Debussy	(1862 - 1918)
Leonard Bernstein	(1918 - 1990)

Jazz Pioneers

Louis Armstrong	1901
Duke Ellington	1899
John Coltrane	1926
Thelonious Monk	1917
Dizzy Gillespie	1917
Miles Davis	1926
Charlie Parker	1920
Art Blakey	1919

Pioneer Rock Bands

The Rolling Stones

The Beatles

The Who

The Kinks

Jimi Hendrix

Cream

Led Zeppelin

Black Sabbath

Deep Purple

Glossary of Musical Terms

A

Absolute music: instrumental music with no intended story (non-programmatic music).

A cappella: choral music with no instrumental accompaniment.

Accelerando: gradually speeding up the speed of the rhythmic beat.

Accent: momentarily emphasizing a note with a dynamic attack.

Adagio: a slow tempo.

Allegro: a fast tempo.

Alto: a low-ranged female voice; the second lowest instrumental range.

Andante: moderate tempo (a walking speed; "Andare" means to walk).

Aria: a beautiful manner of solo singing, accompanied by orchestra, with a steady metrical beat.

Art-music: a general term used to describe the "formal concert music." traditions of the West, as opposed to "popular" and "commercial music" styles.

Art song: (genre) a musical setting of artistic poetry for solo voice accompanied by piano (or orchestra).

Atonality: modern harmony that intentionally avoids a tonal center (has no apparent home key).

Augmentation: lengthening the rhythmic values of a fugal subject.

Avant-garde: ("at the forefront") a French term that describes highly experimental modern musical styles.

B

Ballet: (genre) a programmatic theatrical work for dancers and orchestra.

Bar: a common term for a musical measure.

Baritone: a moderately low male voice; in range between a tenor and a bass.

Baroque Era: c1600-1750; a musical period of extremely ornate and elaborate approach to the arts.

This era saw the rise of instrumental music, the invention of the modern violin family and the creation of the first orchestras (Vivaldi, Handel, JS Bach).

Bass: the lowest male voice (see Double Bass).

Bass drum: the lowest-sounding, non-pitched percussion instrument.

Basso continuo: the back-up ensemble of the Baroque Era usually comprised of a keyboard instrument (harpsichord or organ) and a melodic stringed bass instrument (viol' da gamba or cello).

Bassoon: the lowest-sounding regular instrument of the woodwind family (a double-reed instrument).

Beat: a musical pulse.

Bebop: a complex, highly-improvisatory style of jazz promoted by Charlie Parker in the 1940s-50s.

"Big Band" jazz: see "Swing"

Binary form: a form comprised of two distinctly opposing sections ("A" vs. "B").

Bitonality: modern music sound in two different keys simultaneously.

Blues: a melancholic style of Afro-American secular music, based on a simple musical/poetic form. Delta blues began in the early 1900s, "Classic" blues in the late 1920s, "Rhythm and Blues" in the 1940s.

Brass instrument: a powerful metallic instrument with a mouthpiece and tubing that has to be blown into by the player, such as trumpet, trombone, French horn, tuba, baritone, bugle.

C

Cadence: a melodic or harmonic punctuation mark at the end of a phrase, major section or entire work.

Cadenza: an unaccompanied section of virtuosic display, played by a soloist in a concerto.

Canon: a type of strict imitation created by strict echoing between a melodic "leader" and subsequent "follower(s)."

Cantata: (genre) a composition in several movements, written for chorus, soloist(s) and orchestra; traditionally, these are religious works.

Cello: the tenor-ranged instrument of the modern string family (an abbreviation for violoncello).

Chamber music: (genre) music performed by a small group of players (one player per part).

Chant: (genre) a monophonic melody sung in a free rhythm (such as "Gregorian" chant of the Roman Catholic Church).

Character piece: (genre) a 1-movement programmatic work for a solo pianist.

Chimes: a percussion instrument comprised of several tube-shaped bells struck by a leather hammer.

Chorale: 1) a Lutheran liturgical melody; 2) a 4-part hymn-like chorale harmonization.

Chord: a harmonic combination that has three or more pitches sounding simultaneously.

Chorus: 1) a large choral group; 2) in Jazz, a single statement of the main harmonic/melody pattern.

Chromaticism: 1) harmonic or melodic movement by half- step intervals 2) harmony that uses pitches beyond the central key of a work.

Clarinet: the tenor-ranged instrument of the woodwind family (a single-reed).

Classic Era: c1750-1820; a politically turbulent era focused on structural unity, clarity and balance. (Haydn, Mozart, Beethoven).

Coda: (means "tail" in Italian) a concluding section appended to the end of a work.

Collegium musicum: a university ensemble dedicated to the performance of early music (pre- 1750).

Concert band: a large (non-marching) ensemble of woodwind, brass and percussion instruments.

Concerto: (genre) the general term for a multi-movement work for soloist(s) and orchestra (see "solo Concerto" and "concerto grosso").

Concerto grosso: (genre) a 3-movement work for a small group of soloists and orchestra.

Conductor: the leader of a performing group of musicians.

Consonance: pleasant-sounding harmony.

Contrabassoon: the lowest-sounding double-reed instrument of the woodwind family.

Cornet: a mellow-sounding member of the trumpet family.

Countermelody: a secondary melodic idea that accompanies and opposes a main thematic idea.

Counterpoint: a complex polyphonic texture combining two or more independent melodies.

Crescendo: gradually getting louder.

Cymbals: percussion instrument usually consisting of two circular brass plates struck together as a pair.

D

Da capo: (Italian "to the head") a written indication telling a performer to go back to the start of a piece.

Decrescendo: gradually getting quieter (see diminuendo).

Development: 1) The central dramatic section of a sonata form that moves harmonically through many keys 2) The process of expanding or manipulation a musical idea.

Diatonic: a melody or harmony based on one of the seven- tone major or minor Western scales.

Diminuendo: gradually getting quieter (see decrescendo).

Diminution: the shortening of the note values of a theme (usually to render it twice as fast).

Disjunct: a melody that is not smooth in contour (has many leaps).

Dotted note: a written note with a dot to the right of it (the dot adds half the rhythmic duration to the note's original value).

Double bass: the lowest-sounding instrument of the modern string family.

Downbeat: the first beat of a musical measure (usually accented more strongly than other beats).

Duple meter: a basic metrical pattern having two beats per measure.

Dynamics: the musical element of relative musical loudness or quietness.

E

English horn: a tenor oboe; a richly nasal-sounding double-reed woodwind instrument.

Ensemble: a group of musical performers.

Episode: an intermediary (contrasting) section of a Baroque fugue or Classic rondo form.

Equal temperament: the standard modern tuning system in which the octave is divided into twelve equal "half- steps."

Etude: (French) a "study" piece, designed to help a performer master a particular technique exposition: 1) The opening section of a fugue 2) The opening section of a Classic sonata form (in which the two opposing key centers are exposed to the listener for the first time).

Expressionism: an ultra-shocking, highly dissonant modern style of music.

F

Falsetto: a vocal technique that allows a male to sing in a much higher, lighter register (by vibrating only half of the vocal cord).

Flat sign: (b) a musical symbol that lowers the pitch one half-step.

Flute: a metal tubular instrument that is the soprano instrument of the standard woodwind family.

Form: the elemental category describing the shape/design of a musical work or movement.

Film music: (genre) music that serves either as background or foreground material for a movie.

Forte: (f) a loud dynamic marking.

Fortepiano: an early prototype of the modern piano (designed to play both "loud" and "quiet").

Fortissimo: (*f*) a very loud dynamic marking.

French horn: a valved brass instrument of medium/ medium-low range (alto to bass).

Fugue: a complex contrapuntal manipulation of a musical subject.

G

Genre: a category of musical composition (the specific classification of a musical work).

Glissando: a rapid slide between two distant pitches.

Glockenspiel: a pitched-percussion instrument comprised of metal bars in a frame struck by a mallet.

Gong: (also called "tam-tam") a non-pitched percussion instrument made of a large metal plate struck with a mallet.

Grave: a slow, solemn tempo.

Gregorian chant: (genre) monophonic, non-metered melodies set to Latin sacred texts.

H

Half step: the smallest interval in the Western system of equal temperament.

Harmony: the elemental category describing vertical combinations of pitches.

Harp: a plucked instrument having strings stretched on a triangular frame.

Harpsichord: an ancient keyboard instrument whose sound is produced by a system of levered picks, that pluck its metal strings (common in the Renaissance and Baroque eras).

Home key: see tonic key.

Homophonic texture: 1) A main melody supported by chord 2) A texture in which voices on different pitches sing the same words simultaneously.

Horn: see French horn.

I

Idée fixe: a transformable melody that recurs in every movement of a multi-movement work.

Imitation: a polyphonic texture in which material is presented then echoed from voice to voice.

Impressionism: a modern French musical style based on blurred effects, beautiful tone colors and fluid rhythms (promoted by Debussy around the turn of the 1900s).

Improvisation: "on-the-spot" creation of music (while it is being performed).

Incidental music: (genre) music performed during a theatrical play.

Instrumentation: the combination of instruments that a composition is written for.

Interval: the measured distance between two musical pitches.

Inversion: a variation technique in which the intervals of a melody are turned upside down.

J

Jazz: (genre) a style of American modern popular music combining African and Western musical traits.

Jazz band: an instrumental ensemble comprised of woodwinds (saxophones and clarinets), brasses (trumpets and trombones) and rhythm section (piano/guitar, bass and drum set).

K

Kettledrums: see timpani.

Key: the central note, chord or scale of a musical composition or movement.

Key signature: a series of sharps or flats written on a musical staff to indicate the key of a composition.

Keyboard instrument: any instrument whose sound is initiated by pressing a series of keys with the fingers; piano, harpsichord, organ, synthesizer are the most common types.

L

Largo: a very slow, broad tempo.

Legato: a smooth, connected manner of performing a melody.

Leitmotif: a short musical "signature tune" associated with a person or concept in a Wagnerian Music drama.

Libretto: the sung/spoken text of an opera.

Lied: (genre) a German-texted art song (usually for one voice with piano accompaniment); plural: Lieder.

Lute: an ancient pear-shaped plucked instrument widely used in the Renaissance and Baroque eras.

M

Madrigal: (genre) a composition on a short secular poem, sung by a small group of unaccompanied singers (one on a part). The madrigal flourished in Italy from 1520 to 1610, and was adopted in England during the Elizabethan Age (c. 1600).

Major Key: music based on a major scale (traditionally considered "happy" sounding).

Major scale: a family of seven alphabetically ordered pitches within the distance of an octave, following an intervallic pattern matching the white keys from "C" to "C" on a piano).

Marching band: a large ensemble of woodwinds, brass, and percussion used for entertainment at sporting events and parades (usually performing march-like music in a strong duple meter).

Mass: (genre) in music, a composition based on the five daily prayers of the Roman Catholic Mass Ordinary: Kyrie, Gloria, Credo, Sanctus, Agnus Dei.

Mass Ordinary: the five daily prayers of the Catholic.

Mass Proper: the approximately two dozen prayers of a Mass that change each day to reflect the particular feast day of the liturgical calendar.

Marimba: a pitched percussion instrument comprised of wooden bars struck by mallets; a mellower version of the xylophone.

Mazurka: a type of Polish dance in triple meter, sometimes used by Chopin in his piano works.

Measure: a rhythmic grouping, set off in written music by a vertical bar line.

Medieval: a term used to describe things related to the Middle Ages (c450-1450).

Melisma: a succession of many pitches sung while sustaining one syllable of text.

Melody: the musical element that deals with the horizontal presentation of pitch.

Meter: beats organized into recurring and recognizable accent patterns (2/4, 3/4, 4/4, etc.).

Metronome: a mechanical (or electric) device that precisely measures tempo.

Measure: a rhythmic grouping, set off in written music by a vertical bar line.

Mezzo-: an Italian prefix that means "medium."

Mezzo forte: (F) a medium loud dynamic marking.

Mezzo piano: (f) a medium quiet dynamic marking.

Mezzo-soprano: a dramatic woman's voice that combines the power of an alto with the primary high range of a soprano.

Microtone: a non-Western musical interval that is smaller than a Western half step.

Middle Ages: c450-1450; an era dominated by Catholic sacred music, which began as simple chant but grew in complexity in the 13th to 15th centuries by experiments in harmony and rhythm. (Anonymous monks, Pérotin, Machaut).

Minimalism: a modern compositional approach promoted by Glass, Reich, etc., in which a short melodic/ rhythmic/harmonic idea is repeated and gradually transformed as the basis of an extended work.

Minor key: music based on a minor scale (traditionally considered "sad" sounding).

Minor scale: a family of seven alphabetically-ordered pitches within the distance of an octave, following an intervallic pattern matching the white keys from "A" to "A" on a piano).

Minuet: an aristocratic dance in 3/4 meter.

Minuet and **trio form**: the traditional third-movement form of the Classic 4-movement design, based on an aristocratic dance in 3/4 meter.

Mode: a scale or key used in a musical composition (major and minor are modes, as are ancient modal scales found in Western music before c.1680.

Moderato: a moderate tempo.

Modern Era: c1890-present; a musical era impacted by daring experimentation, advances in musical technology, and popular/non-Western influences. (Debussy, Schoenberg, Stravinsky, Copland, Cage).

Modulation: the process of changing from one musical key to another.

Monophonic texture: a single-line texture with no harmony.

Motet: a polyphonic vocal piece set to a sacred Latin text that is NOT from the Roman Catholic Mass.

Motive: a small musical fragment ("Lego" block) used to build a larger musical idea; can be reworked in the course of a composition (as in the 4-note motive in Beethoven's Symphony No. 5 in C minor) movement: a complete, independent division of a larger work.

Musikdrama: (genre) a type of ultra-dramatic German operatic theatre developed by Richard Wagner in the mid-/ late- Romantic era.

Musique concréte: (genre) music comprised of natural sounds that are recorded and/or manipulated electronically or via magnetic tape; a compositional approach promoted by Varèse in the 1950s mute: a device used to muffle the tone and volume of an instrument.

N

Nationalism: musical styles that include folk songs, dances, legends, language, or other national imagery relating to a composer's native country natural sign: (n) a musical symbol that raises the pitch one half-step.

Neo-classicism: an early 20th-century compositional style in which Classic forms and the aesthetics of balance, clarity, and structural unity are combined with modern approaches to harmony, rhythm and tone color.

New age: a style of popular music in the 1980s/90s that rejected the hard-edged beat of rock music by focusing on nature sounds, sweet synthesized tone colors, acoustic instruments, and short hypnotically repetitive ideas.

Nocturne: (French for "night piece") a type of character piece for solo piano that evokes the moods and images of nighttime.

Non-metrical: music without a regular beat or steady meter (you cannot tap your foot to the beat).

Notation: a system for writing music down so that critical aspects of its performance can be recreated accurately.

Note: in music notation, a black or white oval-shaped symbol (with or without a stem/flag) that represents a specific rhythmic duration and/or pitch.

O

Oboe: a nasal-sounding double-reed instrument that is the alto of the standard woodwind family.

Octave: a musical interval between two pitches in which the upper pitch vibrates twice as fast as the lower.

Opera: (genre) a large-scale, fully-staged dramatic theatrical work involving solo singers, chorus and orchestra.

Opera buffa: (genre) comic Italian opera (usually in 2 acts).

Opera seria: (genre) serious Italian opera (usually in 3 acts).

Oratorio: (genre) a large-scale sacred work for solo singers, chorus and orchestra that is NOT staged.

Orchestra: a large instrumental ensemble comprised of strings, woodwinds, brasses and percussion.

Orchestration: the technique of conceiving or arranging a composition for orchestra Ordinary (see "Mass Ordinary").

Organ: a wind/keyboard instrument, usually with many sets of pipes controlled from two or more manuals (keyboards), including a set of pedals played by the organist's feet (a set of mechanical or electrical "stops" allow the player to open or close the flow of air to selected groups of pipes).

Organum: (genre) a type of early French Medieval polyphony dating from c. 1000-1200, featuring a slow non- metered chant in the lowest voice with one or more faster metrical voices sung above (in melismatic style—many notes sung on each syllable of text).

Ostinato: a short rhythmic/melodic idea that is repeated exactly over and over throughout a musical section or work.

Overture: (genre) a one-movement orchestral introduction to an opera (Wagner, Bizet, and other composers after 1850 use the term prelude instead to show dramatic unity between the overture and the theatrical drama that follows it).

P

Pentatonic scale: a folk or non-Western scale having five different notes within the space of an octave.

Percussion instrument: an instrument on which sound is generated by striking its surface with an object.

Phrase: a small musical unit (sub-section of a melody) equivalent to a grammatical phrase in a sentence.

Pianissimo: (π) a very quiet dynamic marking.

Piano: (dynamic; p) a quiet dynamic marking.

Piano: (instrument) a versatile modern keyboard instrument that makes sound via fingered keys that engage felt-tipped hammers that strike the strings.

Pianoforte: the original instrumental prototype of the piano (late Baroque/early Classic eras).

Pitch: the relative highness or lowness of a musical sound (based on frequency of vibration).

Pizzicato: usually refers to a type of violin playing in which a string is plucked by the fingers.

Phrase: a small musical unit (sub-section of a melody) equivalent to a grammatical phrase in a sentence.

Polonaise: A Polish nationalistic military dance used in some of Chopin's piano character pieces.

Polyphony: music with two or more sounds happening simultaneously.

Polyphonic texture: when two or more independent melodic lines are sounding at the same time.

Polyrhythm: when several independent rhythmic lines are sounding at the same time.

Polytonality: when music is played in two or more contrasting keys at the same time.

Postlude: a concluding section (usually at the end of a keyboard movement).

Prelude: (genre) 1) A free-form introductory movement to a fugue or other more complex composition 2) A term used instead of overture (by Wagner, Bizet and other later Romantic composers) to show dramatic unity between the introductory orchestral music and the theatrical drama that follows it.

Prepared piano: a modern technique invented by John Cage in which various natural objects (spoons, erasers, screws, etc.) are strategically inserted between the strings of a piano, in order to create unusual sounds.

Presto: a very fast tempo.

Program music [or "programmatic music"]: (genre) instrumental music intended to tell a specific story, or set a specific mood or extra-musical image.

Program symphony: (genre) a programmatic multi- movement work for orchestra.

Progression: a series of chords that functions similarly to a sentence or phrase in written language.

Proper (Mass): see Mass Proper.

Q

Quadruple meter: a basic metrical pattern having four beats per measure.

Quotation music: (genre; common since c. 1960) a composition extensively using quotations from earlier works.

R

Ragtime: a style of piano music developed around the turn of the 20th century, with a march-like tempo a syncopated right-hand melody, and an "oom-pah" left-hand accompaniment.

Range: the distance between the lowest and highest possible notes of an instrument or melody.

Rap: (hip-hop) a style of popular music developed by Afro- Americans in the 1970s, in which the lyrics are spoken over rhythm tracks.

Recapitulation: the third aspect of Classic sonata form; in this section, both themes of the exposition are restated in the home key (the second theme gives up its opposing key center).

Recitative: a speech-like style of singing with a free rhythm over a sparse accompaniment.

Recorder: an ancient wooden flute.

Reed: a flexible strip of cane (or metal) that vibrates in the mouthpiece of a wind instrument.

Register: a specific coloristic portion of an instrumental or vocal range.

Renaissance: c1450-1600; an era that witnessed the rebirth of learning and exploration. This was reflected musically in a more personal style than seen in the Middle Ages. (Josquin Desprez, Palestrina, Weelkes).

Requiem Mass: (genre) a Roman Catholic Mass for the dead.

Retrograde: a melody presented in backwards motion retrograde inversion: a melody presented backwards and intervalically upside down.

Rhythm: the element of music as it unfolds in time **Rhythm** and **blues**: a style of Afro-American popular music that flourished in the 1940s-60s; a direct predecessor to rock and roll.

Ritardando: gradually slowing down the tempo,

Ritornello form: a Baroque design that alternates big vs. small effects (tutti vs. solo); usually the tutti section is a recurring melodic refrain.

Rock and **roll**: a style of popular music that emerged in the 1950s out of the combination of Afro-American, Country-Western and pop-music elements

Romantic Era: c1820-1890; an era of flamboyance, nationalism, the rise of "superstar" performers, and concerts aimed at middle-class "paying" audiences. Orchestral, theatrical and soloistic music grew to spectacular heights of personal expression. (Schubert, Berlioz, Chopin, Wagner, Brahms, Tchaikovsky).

Rondo form: a Classic form in which a main melodic idea returns two or three times in alternation with other melodies (ABACA or ABACABA, etc.)

Rubato: a flexible approach to metered rhythm in which the tempo is sped up or slowed down at will for greater personal expression.

S

Sackbut: an ancient brass instrument; ancestor to the trombone.

Saxophone: a family of woodwind instruments with a single reed and brass body; commonly used in jazz and marching band/concert band music.

Scale: a family of pitches arranged in an ascending/ descending order.

Scat singing: a style of improvised jazz sung on colorful nonsense syllables.

Scherzo: a country dance in triple meter.

Scherzo and **trio form**: a musical movement based on a country dance in triple meter; replaced the aristocratic minuet in the early 1800s as the usual third movement of the Classic 4-movement design sequence: the immediate repetition of a melodic passage on a higher or lower pitch level.

Score: written notation that vertically aligns all instrumental/vocal parts used in a composition.

Serenade: (genre) a Classic instrumental chamber work similar to a small-scale symphony; usually performed for social entertainment of the upper classes.

Serialism: a method of modern composition in which the twelve chromatic pitches are put into a numerically ordered series used to control various aspects of a work (melody, harmony. tone color, dynamics, instrumentation, etc.) Sharp sign: (#) a musical symbol that raises the pitch one half-step.

Shawm: An ancient double-reed woodwind instrument.

Sforzando (ß): sudden stress on a note or chord.

Singspiel: (genre) a traditionally low-level type of comic light opera, featuring spoken German dialogue interspersed with simple German songs.

Snare drum: a non-pitched drum with two heads stretched over a metal shell; the lower head has metal wires strapped across it to produce a rattling sound.

Solo concerto: (genre) a 3-movement work for a single soloist vs. an orchestra.

Sonata: (genre) a Classic multi-movement work for a piano (or for one instrument with piano accompaniment).

Sonata form (also called sonata-allegro form): the common first-movement form of Classic multi-movement instrumental works; essentially a musical debate between two opposing key centers characterized by three dramatic structural divisions within a single movement: Exposition (two opposing keys are presented), Development (harmonically restless), Recapitulation (all material is presented in the home key).

Sonata-rondo form: a formal design that combines aspects of sonata form and rondo form: (an ABACABA design in which the opening ABA=exposition (two opposing keys presented in "A" vs. "BA"); C=development (harmonically restless); the last ABA=recapitulation (all material is presented in the home key).

Song: (genre) a small-scale musical work that is sung (a German song is a "Lied"; a French song is a "chanson"; an Italian song is a "canzona").

Song cycle: (genre) a set of poetically unified songs (for one singer accompanied by either piano or orchestra.

Soprano: 1) The highest ranged woman's voice or a high pre-pubescent boy's voice; 2) The highest-sounding instrument of an instrumental family.

Sprechstimme: a half-spoken, half-sung style of singing on approximate pitches, developed by Schoenberg in the early 1900s.

Staccato: short, detached notes.

String instrument: an instrument that is played by placing one's hands directly on the strings, such as violin, viola, cello, double bass, harp, guitar, dulcimer, psaltery, and the ancient viols.

String quartet: 1) A chamber ensemble of two violins, viola and cello, devised in the early Classic era 2) A multi-movement work (genre) for two violins, viola and cello.

Strophic form: a song form featuring several successive verses of text sung to the same music.

Subject: the main melodic idea of a fugue.

Suite: (genre) a collection of dance movements.

Swing: a term to describe "Big Band" jazz music of the 1930s-50s.

Symphonic poem: (genre) a single-movement programmatic work for orchestra.

Symphony: (genre) a multi-movement work for orchestra.

Syncopation: an "off-the-beat" accent.

Synthesizer: a modern electronic keyboard instrument capable of generating a multitude of sounds.

T

Tempo: the speed of the musical beat.

Tenor: a high-ranged male voice.

Ternary form: ABA design (statement, contrast, restatement).

Texture: the element focusing on the number of simultaneous musical lines being sounded.

Theme: the main self-contained melody of a musical composition.

Theme and **variations form**: a theme is stated then undergoes a series of alterations.

Through composed form: a song form with no large-scale musical repetition.

Timbre: another term for tone color.

Timpani: various-sized kettle-shaped pitched drums; a tenor instrument of the percussion family.

Tone color: the unique, characteristic sound of a musical instrument or voice.

Tone cluster: a modern technique of extreme harmonic dissonance created by a large block of pitches sounding simultaneously.

Tonality: music centered around a "home" key (based on a major or minor scale).

Tone row: an ordered series of twelve chromatic pitches used in serialism.

Tonic: the first note of a scale or key.

Tonic key: the "home" key of a tonal composition.

Transition: a bridge section between two musical ideas.

Transposition: shifting a piece to a different pitch level.

Tremolo: rapid repetition of a pitch (i.e.: bowing a string rapidly while maintaining a constant pitch).

Triad: a three-note chord built on alternating scales steps (1-3-5, etc.).

Trill: rapid alternation of two close pitches to create a "shaking" ornament on a melodic note.

Trio sonata: (genre) a Baroque multi-movement chamber work for four performers (2 violins and basso continuo).

Triple meter: a common meter with three beats per measure.

Triplet: a rhythmic grouping of three equal-valued notes played in the space of two (indicated in written music by a "3" above the grouping).

Trombone: a family of brass instruments that change pitch via a moveable slide (alto, tenor and bass versions are common).

Trumpet: a valved instrument that is the soprano of the modern brass family.

Tuba: a large valved brass instrument; the bass of the modern brass family.

Tubular bells: see chimes.

Tutti: (Italian for "all" or "everyone") an indication for all performers to play together.

U

Unison: the rendering of a single melodic line by several performers simultaneously.

Upbeat: the weak beat that comes before the strong downbeat of a musical measure.

V

Variation: the compositional process of changing an aspect(s) of a musical work while retaining others.

Verismo: a style of true-to-life Italian opera that flourished at the turn of the 20th century.

Vibrato: small fluctuations in pitch used to make a sound more expressive.

Viol: an ancient string instrument (ancestor to the modern violin).

Viol' da gamba: a Renaissance bowed string instrument held between the legs like a modern cello.

Viola: the alto instrument of the modern string family.

Violin: the soprano instrument of the modern string family.

Violoncello: the full name of the cello; the tenor instrument of the modern string family.

Vivace: a lively tempo.

Volume: the relative quietness or loudness of an electrical impulse (see dynamics).

W

Waltz: an aristocratic ballroom dance in triple meter that flourished in the Romantic period.

Whole step: an interval twice as large as a half step (Ex.: the distance between C and D on a piano).

Whole-tone scale: a scale made of 6 whole steps that avoids any sense of tonality.

Woodwind instrument: an instrument that produces its sound from a column of air vibrating within a multi-holed tube.

Word-painting: in vocal music, musical gestures that reflect the specific meaning of words; a common aspect of the Renaissance madrigal.

X

Xylophone: a pitched percussion instrument consisting of flat wooden bars on a metal frame that are struck by hard mallets.

About the Author

Ashok G P (B. Music)

Born in Bangalore, India, Ashok G P earned a bachelor's degree in music education (2014) from the Bangalore Conservatory. He has served as the Head of the Music Department at the school and college levels, teaches music as a core subject, and conducts choirs. He has introduced non-music majors to music courses and advocates music appreciation and music education. He is a member of the International Society for Music Education.

His research areas include topics such as musical improvisation and seven-part harmony.

He is a multi-instrumentalist who has 20 years of experience in drumming, and 12 years of experience in Classical Guitar. He is an active live sound engineer, he has performed with many bands across South India spanning many genres such as rock, metal, country, classical, pop, blues, and contemporary to name a few.

www.ingramcontent.com/pod-product-compliance
Lightning Source LLC
LaVergne TN
LVHW041546070526
838199LV00046B/1847